SAT Preparation

The Best Guide To Help achieve An Excellent Score In SAT Exam With Proven Strategies

By

Sherman Brooks

SAT

The information herein is offered for informational purposes solely and is universal as so. The presentation of the information is without contract or any type of guaranteed assurance.

The trademarks that are used are without any consent, and the publication of the trademark is without permission or backing by the trademark owner. All trademarks and brands within this book are for clarifying purposes only and are the owned by the owners themselves, not affiliated with this document.

Contents

Introduction

If you are thinking about applying to higher colleges, you should be aware of the SAT & how it would impact your application.

So, what is an SAT? In the United States, it is 1 of 2 standardized college acceptance examinations. (An ACT is another.) A College Board, a nonprofit organization that also administers a PSAT & the Advanced Placement (AP) scheme, is in charge.

An SAT was first conducted as the college admissions exam in 1926, after being modified from the Army Intelligence test. However, it wasn't until 1933 that the exam gained traction. After Harvard's president began utilizing it to evaluate scholarship candidates, he felt that this was an accurate indicator of cognitive capabilities. By the 1940s, this had been the compulsory exam for all candidates & had been applied to about 300,000 individuals worldwide, thanks to this perception of an SAT.

With the introduction of an ACT in 1959, the SAT's domination in college admissions examination was questioned. Despite being originally less successful than an SAT, & ACT gained traction in the Midwest & mountain states, eventually surpassing SAT to be the most famous college admissions measure in 2010.

The SAT undergone several significant improvements in 2016 because of intensified rivalry from ACT. The test's core objective and format haven't changed (it is still a multiple-choice exam used to determine college admissions), but some elements of its composition & content have. The SAT regained its status as the most common college admissions exam in 2018, indicating that schools would accept the reforms.

The fundamentals of SAT will be established in this guide to assist you in preparing for this critical exam.

Chapter 1: A Brief Introduction to the SAT

An SAT is a college entrance test administered by a College Board & is taken by applicants from all over the United States. It's being used to evaluate a student's vital Reading, writing, & math skills & college preparation.

It's also offered seven times a year & is normally provided on the 1st Saturday of every month at 8:00 a.m. (except for the August test).

The SAT requires 3 hrs & 50 mins to finish with an optional essay. It takes 3 hrs without such an essay. If you are applying for colleges that need it, you can just take this SAT for the Essay. Sign-up for such SAT without that Essay if you don't want to write an essay.

Students usually take the exam in the junior year in high school, with the option to retake this in their senior year. Visit a College Board portal to register & review exam times. You would be allowed to select a nearby test center to attend on a testing day when you sign-up.

Seeing at a mock test is the perfect way to get a feel for an SAT exam.

1.1 Format

The exam is structured as follows:

1. Reading (65 mins for almost 52 questions)

2. Writing & Language (35 mins for around 44 questions)

3. Math with No Calculator (25 mins for around 20 questions)

4. Math with Calculator (55 mins for around 38 questions)

5.

1.2 Scoring

The SAT score comprises two parts: 1) Math, & 2) Reading
& Writing Dependent on Evidence (ERW). Each portion is graded
on a scale of 200-800 points, with 800 representing a perfect
score. As a result, the highest possible overall exam
performance is 1600. You might now be curious what constitutes
a perfect performance. In consideration of any college
admissions numbers, below are few general tips:

- **Ivy League:** more than 1500 (Princeton, MIT, Harvard, Yale, Stanford)

- **Top Tier:** more than 1400 (Tufts, UNC, UCLA, Vanderbilt, USC, Emory, Rice, Carnegie Mellon, Duke)

- **Second Tier:** more than 1300 (UMaryland, GWU, Penn State, Fordham, UT Austin, BU)

- **Third Tier:** more than 1200 (Hofstra, DePaul, other state universities)

- Fourth Tier: Les than 1200

In 2017, the average national SAT score was 1060. The national
average for each segment is also included:

- Evidence-based Reading & Writing: 533

- Math: 527

Well, how are results arrived at? To begin, figure out your mean scores for every segment (Reading, math, writing).

The total number of questions in each segment as mentioned below:

- Reading: 52

- Math: 58

- Writing: 44

Your minimum score for every segment is the cumulative amount of questions you answered correctly.

Assume you got twenty-five questions incorrect in all of the math parts. Your sample score will be 58 minus 25 for a total of 33.

Now that you have a sample score of around 33, you will look up the final score upon that test's curve.

Raw Score (# of correct answers)	Math Section Score	Reading Test Score	Writing and Language Test Score
30	550	26	29
31	560	27	29
32	570	27	30
33	580	28	31
34	580	28	31
35	590	29	32
36	600	29	33

A rough score of 33 results in a total result of 580 on this curve. That'd be your maths grade.

There is an additional stage towards the Evidence-based Reading & Writing Score. When you have your last Reading & Writing score from this curve, sum them up, then multiply by ten. Let's presume you have raw Reading & Writing scores of 30 & 35, respectively. These raw grades result in final Reading & Writing scores of 26 & 32, respectively. The total of all these scores becomes 58 (26 + 32). 580 is the product of multiplying by ten. This is your Reading & Writing Score based on Evidence.

Each test has its curve, which is utilized to compensate for the small differences in complexity between exams. Here are few samples of curves from previous test dates.

1.3 What's tested?

So you know the exam includes Math, Reading, & writing, so what exactly is checked in every section?

Here's a quick rundown:

- **Reading**

    - **Reading comprehension** — Answer multiple-choice amidst various passages from the literature, culture, social sciences, and science (main concept, tone, facts, inferences, vocabulary, details, etc.) ...)

- **Math**

- o **The Heart of an Algebra** — interpreting vector formulas, creating models, modifying & solving equations, sets of the equations, inequalities

- o **Problem Solving & Data Analysis** — word problems, rates, percent, probability, statistics, reading data, linear vs. exponential growth

- o **Passport to some Advanced Math** — synthetic division, exponents & radicals, lines, quadratics, expressions, functions

- o **Additional Topics into Math** — complex numbers, volume, angles, circles, trigonometry, triangles

- **Writing**

  - o **Punctuation** — apostrophes, semicolons, commas, colons, dashes

  - o **Grammar Rules** — tenses, fragments, pronoun reference, subject-verb agreement, run-on sentences, modifiers

  - o **Sentence & Paragraph Structure** — relevance & purpose, combining sentences, supporting Evidence, sentence placement, paragraph transitions, transitions,

  - o Understanding Data

  - o Choosing a right word

- **Essay (optional)**

  - o Read & understand the opinionated speech or article.

- o Write the Essay analyzing how one author makes an article persuasive for her or his use of the reasoning, Evidence, & stylistic/rhetorical elements.

Again, taking a mock test is the easiest approach to get acquainted with an SAT.

1.4 How you can Improve?

Never believe that an SAT is an impossible exam to prepare for. The reality is that much like every other exam you would prepare for in your school, studying for this test helps tremendously. Hundreds of students review exam prep books & take lectures every year to improve by 200-300 marks, based on the standard of the teaching.

You have several opportunities for self-preparation and that there's no one "right path." An exam prep course and maybe any private mentor has helped many people succeed. Others tend to learn independently using a variety of books, including research problems.

Regardless of the different directions, you can follow, there are certain common denominators for students that make significant progress:

- They perform many practice exams.

- They go through the practice exercises, again and again, learning from their errors.

- They put their skills to the test by asking real questions.

Consider the items on the page above to be absolute must-dos.

And, regardless of how you want to improve, it is strongly advised you use the tools in this guide. The reviews have proved to be extremely useful in assisting students in improving their test scores.

Chapter 2: Reading Test

Students would be asked questions similar to those expressed in a vibrant, reflective, evidence-based debate on a Reading Test.

It is important to note:

Try out some reading questions. Now it's your turn.

It's More For the Day-to-Day

A Reading Test concentrates on the core abilities
& understanding of education: what you learned in your high school and what you'll have to achieve in college. It's all about how you are taking in, process, and apply content. What's more, say what? You've been using it for a long time.

It's not just how good you remember statistics and words, but you won't require insider knowledge or flashcards, & you won't have to stay up the whole night cramming.

Quick Facts

1. Many of the questions on the Reading Test are multiple-choice questions & dependent on passages.

2. Any passages have been combined with others.

3. Some passages provide informational visuals like tables, graphs, & charts; however, no math will be needed.

4. Prior knowledge of a particular subject is never put to the test.

5. An Evidence-Based Reading & Writing segment includes your Reading Test.

2.1 What the Reading Test Is Like

You'll learn passages & interpret informative graphics on a Reading Test. After that, you'll use what you've seen to respond to queries.

Any queries need you to find a certain piece of knowledge or a concept. You could, therefore, comprehend whatever that author's words mean. To put it another way, you could read in between lines.

2.2 What you'll Read?

To flourish in college & in your future, you will need to be able to learn in various subjects. You'll still need those qualities to perform better in a Reading Test, which isn't a coincidence.

A Reading Test often contains the following:

A passage from either classic or recent piece in American or international literature.

They were influenced by maybe two passages from a US founding paper or a text from Great Global Conversations. Consider the United States Constitution or any speech by Martin Luther king.

A collection of articles on finance, psychology, sociology, or another social science discipline.

Two scientific passages (or a passage & a pair of passages) look at fundamental principles and advances into Earth science, chemistry, biology, or physics.

What Does a Reading Test Look Like?

There's a lot more to Reading than you would think, & a Reading Test assesses a variety of reading abilities.

Possession of Proof

Some questions would need you to:

- Find Evidence into the passage (or a set of passages) which better supports a prior question's response or acts as the foundation for logical inference.

- Determine how authors justify their arguments with Evidence.

- Find a connection between an informative graphic & the passage in which it is combined.

Words in Context

Many of the questions concentrate on key, often encountered terms & phrases that can be used in texts on various topics. Long after exam day, you'll find these terms in college & the office.

The SAT emphasizes your capacity to:

- Use background cues in the passage to determine which sense of any word or expression would be used.

- Determine how a writer's word choice affects the author's context, style, & sound.

History/Social Studies & Science Analysis

There are passages of literature, social sciences, & science on a Reading Test. You'll be asked some questions that will test the ability to use reading abilities that are most important for success with certain topics. For example, you could learn around an experiment & see questions asking you to complete it:

- Investigate hypotheses.

- Data can be interpreted.

- Know the implications.

Solutions are solely dependent upon that passage's specified or inferred substance.

Chapter 3: Writing Test

An SAT Writing & Language Examination requires you to rewrite passages that have been composed specifically for the exam & contain intentional errors.

It is important to note:

Questions on writing & Language Now it's your turn.

It's More For the Day-to-Day

You'll do 3 items on the Writing & Language Test, which people do most of the time as they write & edit:

1. Reading.

2. Finding mistakes & weaknesses.

3. Fixing them.

The good news is that you already do this stuff if you read and understand your job or collaborate on an article with a peer.

The exam assesses the analytical knowledge you are using to identify and fix problems—the skills you learned in your high school & would use to improve in college.

A Few Quick Facts

- Many of the questions are multiple-choice questions, & they are all dependent on the passages.

- Informational visuals, like tables, graphs, & charts, are used in certain chapters; however, no math would be needed.

- Prior experience of the subject is never put to the test.

- An Evidence-Based Reading & Writing segment includes the Writing & Language Test.

-

3.1 What a Writing & Language Test look Like?

Any questions require a near examination of a single phrase. Others necessitate reading the whole document and deciphering a graphic. For example, you may be asked to pick a statement that corrects the scientific chart misinterpretation or better illustrates the significance of the results.

Any passages you strengthen would be about professions, literature, social sciences, the arts, or technology, ranging from theories to non-fiction narratives.

3.2 What a Writing & Language Test Measures?

The Writing & Language Test includes questions that assess a variety of abilities.

You'll be asked to adjust the way passages produce facts & ideas in questions that measure a command of truth. You may choose a response that clarifies an argumentative point or provides a related supporting context, for example.

Words in the Context

You might be asked to enhance the word used in certain queries. Depending on the text around them, you'll pick the right vocabulary to use. You would aim to enhance the precision and conciseness of a passage, as well as the grammar, design, and sound.

History/Social Studies & Science Analysis

You'll be required to critically read passages on literature, social sciences, & scientific subjects, then make editorial choices to enhance them.

Expression of Thinking

Any queries inquire regarding the organization & effect of a passage. For example, you'll be challenged which vocabulary or structural improvements enhance the clarity of the argument & the cohesiveness of the sentences & paragraphs.

Conventions in Standard English

This guide covers the fundamentals of prose, such as sentence construction, use, & punctuation. Words, verbs, phrases, & punctuation will also be changed. Word tense, subject-verb agreement, parallel construction, & comma use are only a few discussed topics.

Chapter 4: Math Test

An SAT Math Exam encompasses various math skills, including focusing on problem-solving, design, strategic method use, & algebraic structure.

Rather than checking you on any possible math subject, the SAT investigates you to apply the math you'll utilize the most in various contexts. The Math Test questions are structured to represent any problem solving & modeling you'll do in:

- Courses in algebra, science, & social science at the college level

- Your current occupations

- Your private life

For example, to address any questions, you will need to go through multiple measures, & in the actual world, a single measurement seldom suffices.

Some Quick Facts

- Most math questions would be multiple-choice questions, but others, such as grid-ins, will need you to bring up with the solution rather than pick it.

- Math Test with Calculator & Math Test with No-Calculator is the two parts of a Math Test.

- Several questions regarding a particular case appear in certain sections of the exam.

-

Focus

A Math Test would concentrate on the 3 fields of mathematics that are most relevant in a variety of college majors & careers:

The supremacy of the linear equations & systems is the subject of Heart of the Algebra.

Problem Solving & Data Analysis are more about being numerate.

Questions in Passport to some Advanced Math necessitate the manipulation of complicated calculations.

Additional Topics in Math, such as geometry & trigonometry, most applicable to college & job preparation, are often included in a Math Test.

The math test measures fluency.

4.1 A Math Test is a chance to elaborate the Following

Execute procedures in a flexible, precise, effective, & strategic manner.

Identify & use the most effective strategy methods to solve challenges efficiently. This might include inspecting a challenge, looking for a shortcut, or reorganizing the data you've been provided.

Conceptual Understanding

You'll see how much you understand math principles, processes, & relationships. You could be challenged to associate properties of any linear equations, their diagrams, & all contexts they serve, for example.

Applications

These real-world problems need you to evaluate a scenario, decide the necessary elements to fix the problem, mathematically describe the problem, & implement a solution.

4.2 Calculator Use

Calculators are valuable instruments, and knowing how to utilize them & when to utilize them can help you excel after high school. Since the Calculator will save you time on the Math Test with Calculator section of the examination, you'll be completely focused on abstract modeling & reasoning.

A calculator, like any other instrument, is just as wise as the individual who uses it. And if you are required to utilize a calculator on a Math Test, there are certain problems where it is preferable not to. Students who utilize structure or the willingness to think would likely finish ahead of students using a calculator in such situations.

The Math Exam with No Calculator section of the examination allows assessing your math fluency & comprehension of certain math concepts far simpler. It even puts the methodology & number sense to the test.

4.3 Grid-In Questions

While most of the questions on a Math Test are multiple-choice questions, 22 percent of student-created answer questions are considered grid-ins. You'll need to solve the problem & type your responses in grids given on the response sheet rather than selecting the right answer from a collection of choices.

4.4 Gridding-In Answers

- In each column, only one circle should be marked.

- The responses shown by filling into circles would be graded (anything written into boxes outside those circles would not be given credit).

- You'll get credit regardless of which column you start entering your answers in; as much as they're registered inside a grid area, you will get credit.

- Only positive numbers & zero are allowed in the grid, which can only contain 4 decimal places.

- Until the issue specifies differently, responses should be entered as decimal or fraction on a grid.

- It is not necessary to reduce the fractions to the simplest form.

- Before entering any mixed numbers into the grid, they must be translated to improper fractions.

- Students should grid a correct amount the grid can handle if the response is the repeating decimal.

A preview of the directions students can see on the exam is seen below.

Answer: $\dfrac{7}{12}$

Write answer in boxes. →

← Fraction line

Grid in result. →

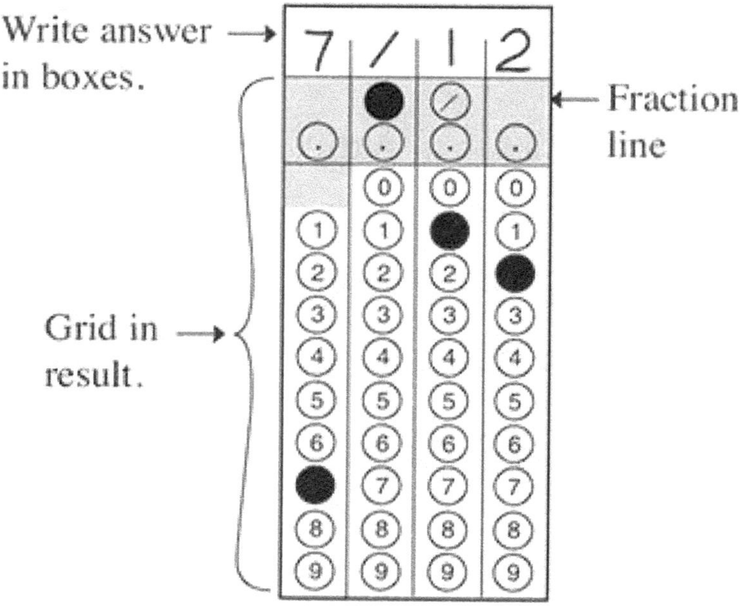

Answer: 2.5

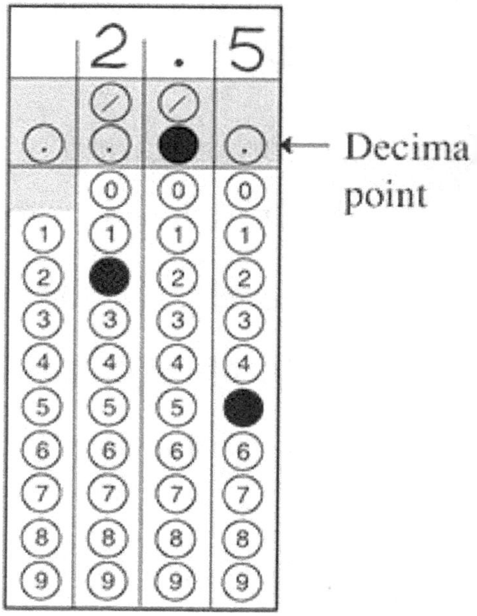

← Decimal point

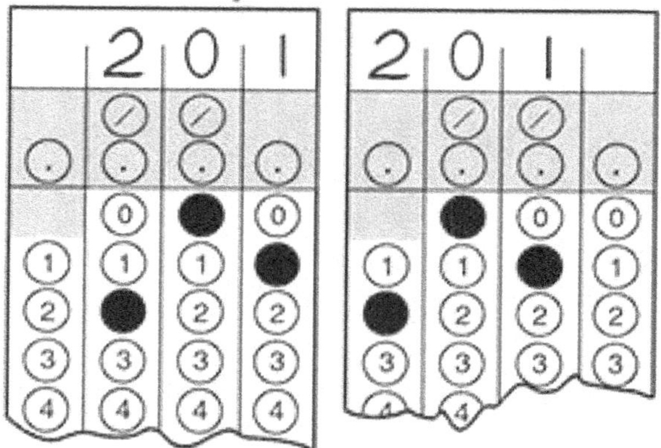

Answer: 201
Either position is correct.

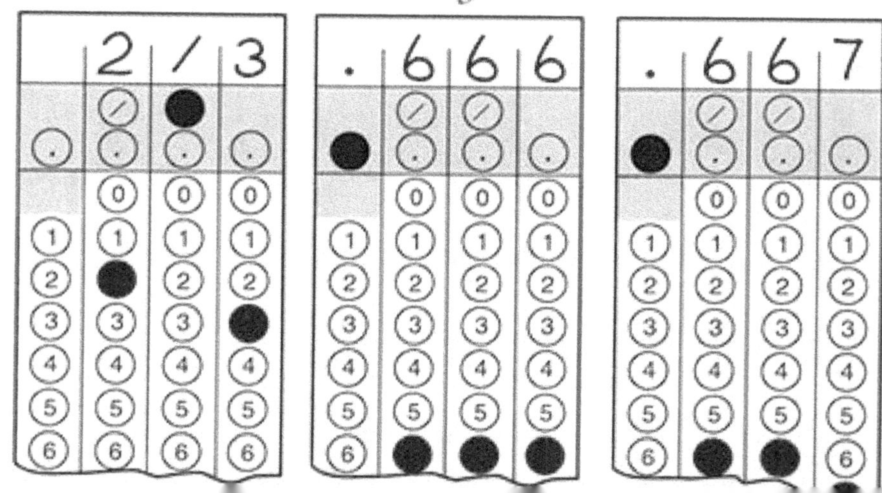

Acceptable ways to grid $\dfrac{2}{3}$ are:

Chapter 5: SAT Essay

The revised SAT Essay tests your ability to learn, analyze, & write.

An SAT Essay is similar to a traditional college writing assignment in which you'd interpret a letter. Take that SAT with the Essay to convince universities that you're able to write on campus.

5.1 What You'll Do?

- Read a section of the book.

- Demonstrate how the speaker constructs a case to convince a reader.

- Use facts from a passage to back up the argument.

5.2 What's New?

The essay portion of an SAT has been fully revamped:

1. It's not required for all colleges, although some are.

2. You have fifty mins to finish the Essay, which is 25 mins longer than an old SAT's mandatory Essay.

3. You will not be required to disagree or agree with a point of view on a subject, nor will you be expected to describe any personal experiences.

5.3 The Essay Prompt

The prompt shown below, or a nearly equivalent one, is used any time the SAT is given.

Remember if [the author] supports assertions with proof, such as statistics or illustrations, as you read the passage below.

- To back up statements, use proof such as statistics or illustrations.

- To generate ideas and link arguments and proof, use logic.

- Stylistic or motivational features, such as word use or emotional appeals, give the concepts articulated more weight.

Write an article describing how [An author] constructs a case to convince [his/her] reader the [author's claim]. Analyze how [that author] strengthens the reasoning & persuasiveness of [his] case by using one or all features mentioned above (or aspects of one's own choice) in your article. Make sure the review reflects on a passage's most important elements. Your article can clarify how an author constructs a case to convince [his/her] readers, not if you comply with [that author's] arguments.

5.4 The Topic

Whenever you take your SAT along with Essay, you'll observe a similar prompt; however, a passage would be different each time.

There are a few elements that both passages have in common:

- Written to appeal to a wide range of people.

- Make a case.

- Subtle opinions on difficult topics are expressed.

- To back up the points, use logic & proof.

Examine theories, controversies, or developments inside the arts & sciences and civic, educational, & political existence. All of the material you'll need to compose your article would be in a passage or into the notes regarding it.

5.5 What an SAT Essay Measures?

An SAT Essay demonstrates your ability to comprehend the passage & use hist as the foundation for the well-written, well-considered debate. In these three groups, the 2 people who grade your Essay can give 1 to 4 points:

Reading: A good essay demonstrates that you comprehended the passage & how key concepts & critical facts interact. It also demonstrates how to utilize textual data effectively.

Analysis: A strong essay demonstrates the interpretation of how a speaker constructs a case by:

- Examining an author's usage of proof, logic, other stylistic & convincing techniques

- Using well-chosen proof from a passage to support & establish arguments

Writing: A good essay is concentrated, ordered, precise, with the style & tone that differs sentence structure & adheres to traditional written English conventions.

Examine SAT Essay guidelines, or rubric, which scorers are using to grade each Essay.

5.6 Who must take an SAT with the Essay?

You are not required to take an SAT with the Essay; however, you would be eligible to submit to the schools that do. Figure out whether an SAT Essay is required or recommended at your level. You should include an SAT with the Essay afterward if you wouldn't apply for it right away.

The expense of an SAT with the Essay is covered by SAT fee waiver.

5.7 Sending Scores

If you appear in an SAT with the Essay, the essay score would be recorded with the other test day scores. And although Score Choice helps you select whether test day's scores to submit to schools, you should never send just a portion of the test day's scores. You can't opt to submit Math scores and not the SAT Essay score, for instance.

Reminder: Check each college's Scores Choice policy before submitting, since certain colleges need you to submit scores from any SAT you've taken. If this seems daunting, bear in your mind that several universities may look for your best work.

The SAT requires a Writing & Language Test, Reading Test, & the Math Test, much as any other tests in an SAT Series of Assessments. Some colleges would include an optional essay section on an SAT. According to a most recent study, SAT questions concentrate on the most important qualities for college preparation & achievement.

5.8 Words in the Context

Many of your SAT questions concentrate on key, often encountered terms & phrases utilized in various texts. Some queries need you to deduce the significance of a term from its context. The terms are those you'll likely hear in college or maybe at work even after the exam is over.

Students can no doubt memories cryptic phrases with flashcards, just to lose them as soon as they set down their exam pencils. The revised tests would encourage students to read closely and recognize the best work produced in the classroom.

5.9 Command of the Evidence

An SAT Essay & an Evidence-Based Reading & Writing portion also need you to analyze, synthesize, & apply Evidence from a variety of sources. Informational illustrations, like tables, charts, & graphs, and multi paragraphs passages in literature & literary non-fiction, the classics, research, culture, & social sciences, & job and job subjects are examples of these outlets.

At a minimum, one query on your Reading Test would require you to classify which section of a text better supports the response to a previous question for each passage or couple of passages you will see. In other cases, you will be required to piece together facts communicated by words & graphics to find the right response to a query.

The Writing & Language Test often emphasizes proof command. It requires you to interpret a sequence of paragraphs or sentences to determine whether they make sense. Other questions need you to analyze graphics & modify a part of the following passage such that the detail within graphics is communicated correctly and reliably.

An SAT Essay often assesses your ability to evaluate facts. Following a reading of the passage, you would be challenged to decide if the author uses facts, logic, stylistic & persuasion devices to convince an audience. Scorers search for well-thought-out, concise analyses backed up with logical reasoning & proof from the document.

5.10 Essay Analyzing the Source

The new SAT Essay requires reading passages to illustrate how a speaker constructs a case to convince an audience. Since you must discuss how well the author utilized proofs, logic, stylistic & convincing features, this challenge is somewhat similar to college writing assignments.

The latest Essay was created to assist high school teachers and students in developing close comprehension, careful examination, and simple writing skills. It would encourage students to read a broad range of arguments & analyze how authors approach their writing.

Any time an SAT is given, the essay prompt would be the same; however, a source material student would be required to write regarding would be different.

While not all students can take an SAT with the Essay, it is required for certain school districts & colleges. The Essay is only used in an SAT as part of an SAT Series.

5.11 Math which Matters Most

Problem Solving & Heart of the Algebra, Data Analysis, & Passport to the Advanced Math are the 3 main fields of math covered in detail on a Math Test.

To be quantitatively literate is important for problem-solving & data analysis. Research, social science, & work backgrounds involve utilizing averages, figures, & proportional logic to solve issues.

A mastery of the linear equations & systems is emphasized in the heart of Algebra, which aids students in developing main abstraction abilities.

Passport to the Advanced Math is on more complicated calculations & the manipulation used to solve them.

According to current studies, these fields are predominantly used across a diverse variety of majors & professions. The new SAT features questions on various math subjects, including the types of geometric & trigonometric abilities that are most useful in college & professions.

5.12 Problems Grounded into Real-World Contexts

All through the SAT, you will be asked a few questions based on real-world experiences that are closely linked to work done in college & in your profession.

Questions on the literature & literary non-fiction are included in an Evidence-Based Reading & Writing portion, as are charts, tables, & passages similar to those used in education, social science, & other majors & professions.

On a Writing & Language Test, you'll be asked to rewrite, update, & develop texts from arts, culture, social education, science, & job backgrounds, among other things.

Multi-step applications for solving problems in physics, social science, work examples, & other real-life issues can be found in your Math section. The test creates a scenario & asks you a series of questions that enable you to delve deeper & model that mathematically.

5.13 Analysis into Science & in Social/History Studies

The updated SAT requires you to use your writing, Language, Reading, & math abilities to address questions in history, science, & social sciences. Therefore, the tests draw on the same types of expertise & skills that you will utilise in college, throughout work, & in your life for making sense of recent political trends, discoveries, world affairs, health & environmental problems.

In an Evidence-Based Reading & Writing area and a Math section, the revised SAT features various demanding texts & informational illustrations that highlight these problems & topics. Reading & understanding texts, revising texts to be compatible with Evidence presented in the graphics, synthesizing knowledge conveyed by texts & graphics, and solving issues based on science & social science would all be needed.

5.14 US Founding Document & Great Global Discussion

On an SAT, you will be prompted to read the quotation from the United States' founding document or a global debate that they sparked.

A founding document of the United States, like a Declaration of the Independence, a Bill of the Rights, & a Federalist Papers, was influenced by and continued to stimulate a discussion regarding the essence of public life that persists.

Authors, speakers, & thinkers from the United States & around the globe, such as Edmund Burke, Nelson Mandela, Mary Wollstonecraft, & Mohandas Gandhi, also helped expand and intensify the debate on important issues, including equality, liberty, & human dignity.

Texts from such a global dialogue are used on the Sit. The aim is to encourage students to read such rich, insightful, and sometimes profound texts closely, not just to learn useful college & job preparation skills but to focus on & actively interact with issues & concerns that are fundamental to informed citizenship.

5.15 No Punishment for Guessing

On an SAT, you win points for correctly answering questions. So go forth and address each query to the best of your ability—no, there's a point in keeping them blank.

Chapter 6: SAT / ACT Prep Guides & Tips

The majority of internet guides on how to get an 800 seem to be of poor consistency. They're mostly published by individuals who have never had an 800. You can normally say because their suggestion is ambiguous and unpractical. Easy Reading tips like "don't neglect to speculate on any topic!" aren't enough.

You will focus on getting 800 throughout this guide. These tactics, though, also apply if your target is 700.

6.1 Understand all Stakes: Why 800 SAT Writing + Reading?

Let's be clear: an SAT score of 1550 or higher is equal to a brilliant 1600. 1590 would not get you extra credit at a top college besides 1550. You've already surpassed their score mark, and the remainder of the application will determine whether or not you are admitted.

So, if you've already had 1550, do not waste your precious time training for 1600. You've already applied to the best schools; now it is time to focus on the remainder of the application.

However, if you have 1540 or lower and choose to attend a best ten college, this is worth taking the time to raise your score to 1550 or higher. The disparity between a 1450 & 1550 is important because 1450 is simpler to obtain (and many applicants do), whereas 1550 is far more difficult.

1540 puts you in the middle of the pack at Harvard, Princeton, & being mediocre is sensitive to the quality of the Ivy League enrollment, where acceptance rates are usually below 10%.

So, why did you get 800 on the SAT Reading+Writing test? Since it allows you to cover for flaws in other areas. In general, schools pay greater attention to your composite performance than to your specific segment results. If you achieve a great 40 on the SAT Reading section, you will get 39 on the SAT Writing section (for a maximum of 790 into Reading+Writing) or a 760 on the SAT Math section & still be assured in the test results. This provides you with a great deal of versatility.

The 75th percentile at Harvard The average for Reading is 780.

In another situation, an 800 on an SAT Reading test is important if you choose to apply to the top school as a social science or humanities student (e.g., political science, English, or communications).

The explanation for this is that academic success is more about comparing candidates. The school needs to accept the brightest because you're up against other students in the "bucket."

If you register as a social science/humanities major, you'll be up against other social science/humanities majors, who would have an easier time with the SAT Reading portion. It's really easy.

Here are some school-based scenarios. The 75th percentile in SAT Reading average for Princeton, Yale, Harvard, & the University of Chicago is 770 or higher. This indicates that a minimum of 25% of the students at such schools has an SAT Reading score of 770.

However, if you really can make your way up to 800, you've shown that you're on target. All that counts is the grade you get in the end, even though it requires much effort.

6.2 Know That You Can Do It

This isn't about a warm and fuzzy greeting on the rear of the Starbucks cup.

You and any other relatively intelligent student are capable of achieving a flawless SAT Reading grade.

Many people don't succeed because they do not try hard or learn correctly.

Even though Language is not your best suit, you should do it, or maybe you just received a B+ for AP English.

And the SAT score reflects how diligently you practice & how much you learn rather than anything else.

6.3 The SAT Reading section is intended to deceive you. You must learn how!

The reason for this is because the SAT seems to be a strange exam. Don't you have the impression that the issues are unlike anything you've had in school as you appear in it?

You've experienced this problem: you often skip questions on the SAT Reading passages due to "unlucky guess." You will try to exclude a few options, & the remaining options would all sound similarly appealing.

Then you raise your hands & guess at random.

As you are researching SAT Reading, this is one of your main concerns, & you realize it affects many of your PrepScholar classmates.

An SAT is purposefully constructed in this manner to perplex you. Millions of students are dealing with the same issue as you. And an SAT is well aware of this.

In most English classes at your school, the instructor can assure you that certain text interpretations are correct. You should compose an essay on anything you like, & English teachers are not permitted to inform you whether your viewpoint is incorrect (usually). That's because asking you what and how to think will get you in trouble, particularly when it comes to complicated problems like poverty or slavery.

The SAT, on the other hand, has a very different problem. This is a national exam, so all students across the globe must compete on an equal footing. It is important to use a reliable test to evaluate students. Any query requires a single, unequivocally right response.

There is always just one right answer. Find your way to get rid of three wrong responses.

Consider what would happen if this were not the case. Assume that every reading response has two possible answers, both of which may be right. When the results were out, any individual student who had answered a question incorrectly complained to a College Board regarding the incorrect exam.

If it is so, a College Board will have to negate the issue, reducing the test's effectiveness.

Every College Board needs to stop a situation like this. As a result, there is only one correct response to each Reading passage query.

However, the SAT hides this truth. It poses problems such as:

1. One of the above points does an author most certainly comply with?

2. The 1st paragraph aims to:

3. 'Dark' in line 20 is almost a synonym:

Is there a trend emerging here? An SAT still hides the reality that there is only one correct response. It attempts to GET you to choose from 2 or 3 of the possible answers.

Then you choose at random.

Then you make a mistake.

It's a safe bet the students would fall for it. Per year, thousands of times.

This is not appreciated by students who do not properly study for SAT. However, if you dress well for your SAT, you would be certain of all SAT tricks. You'll even boost your ranking.

Patterns like some of these abound in an SAT Reading area. You only need to do a few things to raise your ranking:

- Learn how to answer questions like the 1 above on the SAT.

- Learn how to answer these questions utilizing strategies that you already have.

- So that you will benefit from your errors, practice on even a large number of issues.

And if you do not think yourself a competent reader or an excellent English student, you should master these skills. This guide will tell you how you can do it in more depth later.

Last but not least, let's make sure your know how many questions you might skip getting an 800.

What would it take you to Get a 40 in your Reading?

It's easier to grasp what you'll do to get the result on the individual exam if you have got a goal score in your mind. The Reading segment has 52 questions, & the number of questions you skip decides your graded score out from 40.

A raw result to scaled result conversion tables from 4 measures is taken from an Official SAT monk Tests. (Read this if you need a refresher about how an SAT is graded & raw scores were calculated.)

Raw Score	Test 1	Test 2	Test 3	Test 4
52	40	40	40	40
51	40	39	40	39
50	39	38	39	39
49	38	37	38	38
48	38	37	38	37
47	37	36	37	36
46	37	35	36	35
45	36	35	36	35

These grading standards are very strict. If you skip only 1 question on tests 2 & 4, you will get a score of 39. This ensures you will get a top score of 790 in Reading and Writing.

If you skip a question on tests 1 & 3, you'll always get a flawless 40, so if you skip another, you'll get a 39.

The test's complexity determines the scoring graph curve. The curve becomes smoother as the test becomes more difficult. However, you can't know what sort of exam you'll receive on test day.

The best course of action is to strive towards excellence. For 800, you can shoot for a maximum raw score on any practice exercise.

Take notice of the disparity between your current score and the 800 you ought to achieve. For instance, if your raw score is 35, you'll need to get a total of 40 & an 800 by answering 6-7 further questions correctly.

Finally, here's a screenshot of the exact impact assessment from Mar 2014, which shows that a candidate got an 800 despite missing 1 question.

CRITICAL READING: **800**

RANGE

200   800

770 - 800

When you take tests more than once, your scores may vary. This expected variation is considered your score range.

National Percentile: 99%

	TOTAL QUESTIONS	CORRECT ANSWERS	INCORRECT ANSWERS	OMITTED ANSWERS
CRITICAL READING				
SENTENCE COMPLETION	19	19	0	0
PASSAGE-BASED READING	48	47	1	0
TOTAL	67	66	1	0

See page 3 for details on your critical reading score.

(It's from the previous 2400 edition of an SAT, but the grading scale was similar.)

Okay, so you've covered why raising your Reading score is critical, why you're capable of doing so, & a raw score you'll need to reach your goal.

Now you'll get to the root of this guide: actionable tactics & reading suggestions that you must apply to your learning to increase your ranking.

Chapter 7: How to Achieve a Maximum SAT Reading Results?

7.1 Strategy 1: Recognize your high-level weak spot passage or management strategy—and work on it?

Each student requires different SAT Reading flaws. Some individuals lack effective mechanisms for answering passage queries. Others mismanage their time & left with no time before completing all of their questions.

Here's how to find out the one which pertains to you the most:

Taking out the Reading part of the authorized SAT practice examination. The full set of free practice exams can be found here.

Using a timer for each segment, counting down 65 mins for the Reading section. Treat it as though it were a real exam.

If the time limit for that part has expired and you're able to pass forward, do so. Keep going as much as you have to if you are not able to go forward. Have a particular note of "Extra Time" for any new response or answer which you modify.

Once you're ready, rate your exam using the response key and performance table, but keep in mind that you're looking for two scores: 1) Your Realistic performance under standard timing constraints, and 2) your Additional Time score. That's why, during Additional Time, you labeled those questions you replied to or modified.

Can you see where you're going with this? You will work out whatever score you'd get if you had been allowed all the time you wanted by labelling which questions you did during Extra Time. This will assist you in determining the areas of vulnerability.

Your Additional Time performance would be like your Reasonable score if you did not take some extra time.

Did you get 35 or higher on Extra Time?

If you answered NO (Additional Time score less than 35), you have strategy & material issues. You won't be able to get above 35 for all the spare time within the universe, so the 1st line of attack would be to identify & attack your vulnerabilities (you'll go into this later).

If you answered yes (Additional Time score more than 35), you could do the following:

Was it 35 or higher on the Realistic scale?

If the answer is NO (Extra Time more than 35, Realistic less than 35), you have a discrepancy between the Extra Time & Realistic scores. If the gap is greater than three points, you have serious time management issues. You have to find out if this is the case. Are you employing the most effective passage reading tactics? Is it taking you so long to find the answer to each question? In general, practicing many questions & studying the most effective passage tactics will help you save time. There will be more of this later.

If your Extra Time & Realistic scores are greater than 35, you get a decent chance of having an 800. If the difference between the Extra Time & Realistic scores is more than two points, you'll gain from understanding how to perform calculations faster. If not, you'll probably learn from brushing up on the previous material flaws and preventing sloppy errors.

Hopefully, that was clear. Typically, students with both timing & material problems; however, you can notice that one is far more dominant than others for you. For instance, if you could get 40 with additional time but just 35 in standard time, you understand you have to improve your time management skills to get 40.

This study method is so critical that it is indeed a core component of PrepScholar, your exam prep curriculum. When a freshman begins classes, she or he is given a diagnostic to determine basic weaknesses and strengths. The curriculum then adjusts the learning to ensure that you're only training in the areas you can develop the most.

The following tactics would solve all of the vulnerabilities, regardless of what they are.

7.2 Strategy 2: Learn to Eliminate 3 Wrong Answers

This was perhaps the most important technique for improving your Reading grade. It altered your perspective on passage issues.

You spent a bit of time earlier on how an SAT has always had one clear answer. It has a significant impact on the approach you can take to determining the correct SAT Reading response.

Here's another way to look at it: 3 of the 4 solution options have something completely incorrect in them. Just one response is right 100 percent of the time, which suggests the other 3 are incorrect 100 percent of the time.

You understand how you want to remove solution options before you're left with some, which all seem to be similarly probable to be, right? "Well, this might work...however, then again, it might not..."

STOP it right now. You're not minimizing answer options effectively enough. Remember that every bad decision should be crossed for its purposes.

You ought to change the way you think of reading questions. Find a rationale to delete three answer options instead. "Is it possible for you to come up with a justification to exclude this solution option? What do you think of this?"

For each query, you must learn how to exclude three answer options.

It's important to note that a single term will cause an answer option to be incorrect. The SAT has put each term in each possible answer for a specific purpose. Even if most of the response sounds fine, you can delete a word within the answer option if a passage document doesn't accompany it.

The SAT likes to use some classic incorrect answer choices. Here's an illustration of a concern.

Let's say you just finished reading a passage on how social development influenced the world. There are some examples provided. First, it discusses how the change from ancient species such as Homo habitus towards neanderthals resulted in increased tool use, such as fire, which resulted in wildfires & influenced the ecosystem. It also discusses Homo sapiens 40 million years ago & their disappearance in animals such as woolly mammoths due to overhunting.

Then you get to a question like, "Which one of the below better represents the passage's key subject?" The options for answers are mentioned below:

A: The shift from Homo habilus to Neanderthals

B: Evolutionary research

C: The effect of the climate on human development

D: Evolutionary plausibility

E: The effect of human evolution on the environment

(You're using 5 responses for illustration purposes; the SAT would only have 4 options.)

When you read through these options, a couple of them are likely to strike you as extremely probable.

What a pleasant surprise! Any of the responses from A to D contains a significant flaw. Everyone is a typical example of the SAT's wrong response form.

Wrong Answer 1: Too Specific

A: The shift from Homo habilus to Neanderthals

This sort of incorrect response concentrates on a minor aspect of a passage. It's designed to fool you into thinking, "Well, this stated in a passage, so that's a reasonable response option."

That's incorrect! Consider if this solution option accurately describes the whole passage. Is it possible to use it as the passage's title? You'll notice that it's much too vague to express the general point of a passage.

Wrong Answer 2: Too Broad

B: Evolutionary research

This form of incorrect response has an opposite issue: it is much too general. Yes, a passage is technically about evolution, but one element of it, particularly its effect on the climate.

For another absurd scenario, suppose you were talking to a buddy about your mobile phone & he told you that your key argument was all about the world. Well, you were discussing the cosmos, but just a small part of it. It is much too general.

Wrong Answer 3: Reversed Relationship

C: The effect of the climate on human development

Since it contains all of the correct answers, this incorrect response option may be perplexing. The connection between those terms, on the other hand, must be right. In this case, that relationship is reversed. These are the kinds of sloppy errors that people who study so easily create!

Wrong Answer 4: Unrelated Concept

D: Evolutionary plausibility

Finally, this type of incorrect response preys on students' predisposition to overthink your query. If you like debating evolution, this may be a good starting point because every examination about evolution becomes an opportunity to debate its plausibility. Of necessity, this term should not surface in a passage, but certain students may be unable to stop.

Can you see what you are getting at? On the table, each of your response options seems to be a viable option. Any of these answers would seem logical to a less-educated pupil.

However, plausible is not enough. The correct response must be 100 percent correct. You must exclude any incorrect answers that are off even by one letter.

Carry this mindset into any SAT Reading passages query you answer, and it is guaranteed you'll see an increase in your ratings.

7.3 Strategy 3: Predict the Answer before Reading the Answer Choices

An SAT is built to entice you towards making errors by placing very close answer options next to one another, which you've already seen.

You discussed the technique of ruthless, unyielding exclusion of answer options in Technique 2.

Here is a strategy that has proven to be successful for you. Prepare your response to the query before reading your answer options.

Predict the correct response with the crystal ball.

This approach is specifically intended to combat the ambiguity of the solution options.

If you're not using this technique, your thought process would probably go anything like this: " "you just finished reading the question. Response A is unquestionably incorrect. B has the potential to be useful. C...this doesn't quite appeal, but you think it might function." & so on. You've already fallen prey to a College Board's strategy of muddled response options.

Take a different approach. Before reading solution options, emerge with your perfect answer to a query when reading your question. This keeps you from being swayed by an SAT's response choices, especially those that are incorrect.

If the query is a "Big Picture" question regarding the passage's key subject, respond for yourself, "Just what will make a reasonable title for your passage?"

If it is an "Inference" topic, think about what the author might think about the condition described in a question.

And though you can't immediately address the query—for example, whether you need to go back to a line num to recall what a passage was about—try and answer your question while looking through the answer options.

The most important thing to remember is that your passage should help your response option. The passage must explain any correct response on SAT passages; otherwise, your answer will be unclear, causing the problems mentioned earlier with canceling queries.

Warning: this method only works when you can interpret & comprehend passages fluently & have previous experience with the SAT Reading queries. That's why, once you reach the 600 marks, Expert don't suggest using this technique because you're more willing to experiment with the incorrect response option in your mind.

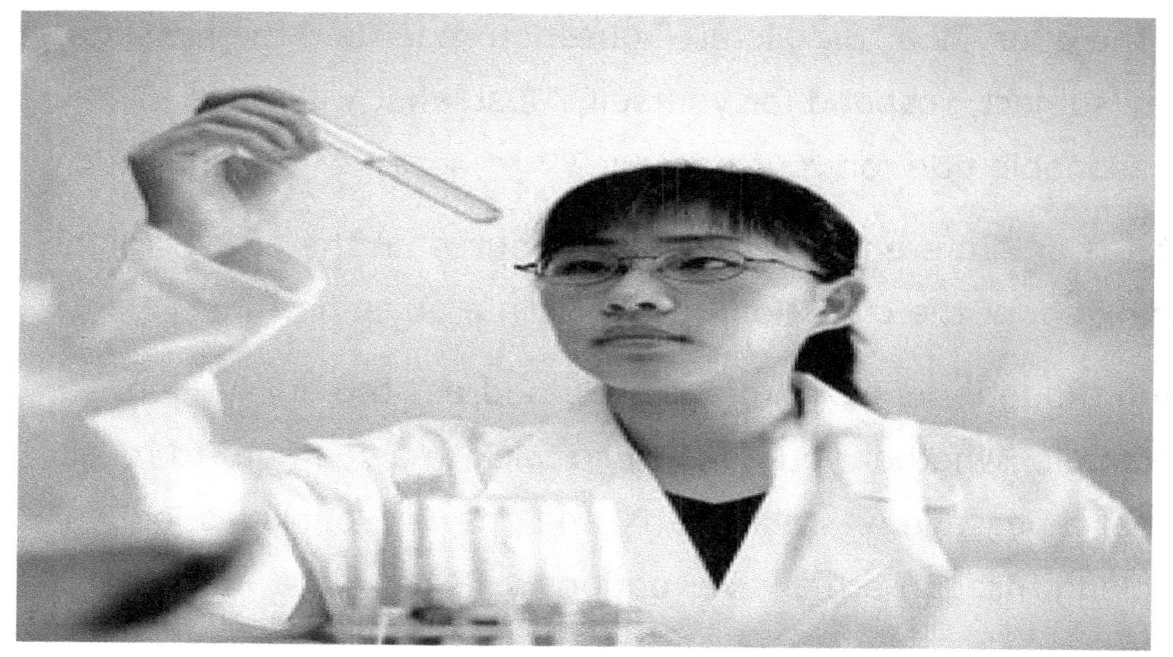

7.4 Strategy 4: Understand Every Mistake You are Making

On the road to excellence, you must ensure that all of the negative points are addressed. It is shown within the score chart above that even one error will bring you down via an 800.

The first move is actually to practice a lot. Whether you're learning from free or book content, you'll need access to millions of practice queries. You have above 7,000 SAT queries personalized to and expertise as a component of your PrepScholar curriculum.

The 2nd — and most crucial — a move is being ruthless in identifying and correcting your errors.

There's an explanation for any error you create on an exam. You can make the same error over & over if you do not understand why you skipped the question.

You've had students take a total of 20 sample exams. They've answered over 3,000 queries, but their SAT Reading average is still far from fine.

What is the reason for this? They were never able to comprehend their errors. They were simply slamming their heads into a wall over & over.

Consider yourself the exterminator because the cockroaches are your faults. You must remove each one—& determine the cause of everyone—or the restaurant where you operate will be closed down.

Here is what you can do:

Label any topic that you are even 20% uncertain about on each practice test or question collection you take.

Check every question you labeled, as well as every inaccurate question while grading the quiz or test. And if you predicted a query wrong, you'll want to go through it again.

Write the following in the notebook:

- #1: a gist of your question,

- #2: why you overlooked it,

- #3: What you will do to stop making the same error again.

Separate parts based on issue (vocab questions, inference questions, big picture queries, etc.).

It isn't enough to consider it and carry it forward. It is not sufficient to simply read the response description. You should consider why you missed this query in particular.

You'll have a running list of any question you skipped & your reflection about why you missed it if you follow this systematic process to your errors.

When it applies to the faults, there are no excuses.

Still, Dig a Little Deeper—How Come You Missed a Reading Query?

What are a few of the more popular explanations for missing a question? "You didn't have this issue correct," don't just suggest. That's a lame excuse.

Often go a little further—what did you forget specifically, & what do you need to work on in the future?

Here are a few popular explanations you may skip a Reading query, as well as how you can go deeper into the analysis:

You couldn't get rid of enough incorrect response options, or you got rid of the right answer.

Further, why wasn't it possible for you to exclude the response option during a test? How do you avoid this kind of response option in your future?

Unscrupulous Error: You misunderstood the query or provided an incorrect answer.

Even further, why would you misunderstand the question? What do you do to stop this in the future?

Vocab: you didn't understand what the main word implied.

Taking it a step further, what was this word? And what's the meaning of the term? Are there any other terms in this paragraph that you're unfamiliar with?

Have you gotten the picture? You're putting a lot of effort into figuring out why you're skipping queries.

Yes, it's difficult, draining, and time-consuming. That is why the vast majority of students who learn inefficiently do not progress.

Many citizens may not understand how to learn properly. Just a small percentage of those who can apply the proper procedures consistently, day in and day out.

You, on the other hand, are special. You've already shown that you value more than most other students by reading that document. You'll also learn more than most students if you implement these ideas and discuss the errors.

Reviewing errors is so critical that within PrepScholar, it is clarified how you can get the right response & why incorrect responses are incorrect with each of the 7,000+ quizzes. That even point out tempting responses so you might understand the SAT's tactics on examinees like you.

When you're going through practice queries, the very first thing you'll do is review the solution description and maybe think about it.

It is a tad too easy. You call passive learning, so you aren't consciously dealing with the error you created.

Instead, attempt something new: find the right response option (A-D) but skip the clarification. Instead, go through the topic again to see if you can find the right response.

This can be difficult at times. Why should you fix it the 2nd time around if you could not solve this the 1st time?

With much fewer time constraints this time, you may see a new excuse to exclude the incorrect response option or whatever may appear. Everything can "click" in your mind.

When this occurs, you will remember what you heard 20 times larger than when you only read a response description. This is everything you've seen firsthand. When you stuck with it & then succeeded, you remember the insight even more than you've learned it passively.

This is ideal for the SAT. Since you'll frequently skip a query due to an erroneous reading of a document, you can read. You'll practice having the correct understanding of a text by pushing yourself to have the correct response. Perhaps better, you will be scouring your passage for hints as to whether the right response is correct; that is precisely what the passage plan requires in the first place.

It's all too simple to read the interpretation of the response and make it go into one ear & out another. You would not benefit from your error because you'll have to make the same mistake.

Treat each incorrect query as though it were a puzzle. Spend almost 10 mins on each incorrect response. If you don't understand, read the response description.

Chapter 8: FAQs About SAT

8.1 When should you take the SAT?

An SAT, ACT, or both were taken by most higher school students, mostly in the spring of the junior year or the fall of the senior year. It's critical to give yourself enough time to retake the exam if you need to improve the score before applying to college. Each year in August, March, May, November, December, October, & June, an SAT is administered nationwide.

8.2 What is on the SAT?

An SAT is divided into two sections:

- Evidence-Based Reading & Writing

- Math

An alternative Essay portion is also included on an SAT. The results of the SAT Essay are recorded separately from the results of the rest of the exam. You could be required to complete an SAT Essay by certain schools. The admissions policy of every college can be found on a school's webpage or in your school profiles.

8.3 How lengthy is an SAT?

An SAT is a three-hour test. An SAT with the Essay would take 3 hrs & 50 mins if you chose this option.

8.4 How is an SAT scored?

An SAT is graded on a scale of 200-800 points for each segment. The number of your segment scores determines your final SAT ranking. The best SAT score available is 1600. You could get a different score if you took the Essay.

8.5 Should you take an SAT or an ACT?

Most colleges & universities recognize scores from both the SAT & the ACT & do not choose one to the other. College-bound students, on the other hand, are gradually taking that both SAT & the ACT. An SAT's 2016 changes have made it simpler than ever before to prepare for all exams simultaneously—and to achieve competitive results on both! Taking a timed, full-length practice test of every form is the easiest way to determine if an SAT, Conduct or both tests are correct for you. Since a SAT & ACT are so close in substance and form, things such as how you approach time pressure & what kinds of questions you find the most difficult will help you figure out which test seems to be a better match. Take mock QUIZ to find out whether you should take the ACT, SAT, or both. and find out more

8.6 How do you register for an SAT?

The deadline to register for the SAT is around 5 weeks before the test date. On the website of the College Board, you may register online. In such conditions, any College Board can request SAT enrollment by mail.

8.7 How can you prep for an SAT?

Experts will assist you. Any student & every budget will benefit from their SAT preparation services.

Conclusion

An SAT is a college entry test that most schools & universities use to determine admissions. A College Board developed & administers an SAT, a pencil-and-paper exam, multiple-choice.

An SAT aims to assess a higher school student's college preparation & provide the college with a single point of comparison for all candidates. Standardized test scores would be evaluated alongside the higher school GPA, subjects taken in higher school, statements of encouragement by extracurricular experiences, coaches or professors, acceptance reviews, & individual essays by university admissions officers. The significance of SAT scores within the college application phase differs by grade.

Overall, the better your SAT & ACT ratings, the more opportunities you'll have for attending & paying for education.